Original title:
Willow Words

Copyright © 2025 Creative Arts Management OÜ
All rights reserved.

Author: Matthew Whitaker
ISBN HARDBACK: 978-1-80567-061-2
ISBN PAPERBACK: 978-1-80567-141-1

Serenity Found Among Whispering Greens

Amidst the leaves where chatter flies,
A squirrel stole my sandwich prize.
He bowed and grinned, a furry clown,
As I just stood there, looking down.

The branches danced, they swayed and spun,
Tickled by breezes, all in fun.
A crow cawed loud, a stand-up act,
With a joke so bad, it lost its tact.

Under the shade, I laid my head,
Imagined cool drinks, a feast instead.
The grass beneath tickled my toes,
Each blade a jester in nature's show.

So here I sit, just laughing wide,
With trees that groan and roots that bide.
Life's quirks abound in nature's court,
Making serenity my favorite sport.

Serenity in Twisting Tendrils

In a garden where the branches sway,
I found a squirrel who wanted to play.
He wore a hat that was far too big,
With a feather stuck from a friendly pig.

The sun peeked through the leaves so green,
While the world below felt like a scene.
The flowers giggled, swaying with glee,
In this quirky place, just you and me.

Softness in the Wind's Embrace

The breezes blow with a tickling tease,
Whispering secrets through playful trees.
A bunny hopped, tripped over a shoe,
And laughed as he rolled, oh what a view!

Clouds above dance in a cotton candy swirl,
While bees buzz loudly, giving a twirl.
A ladybug lounges, sipping hot tea,
In this boisterous place, where funny things be.

Dance of the Graceful Shimmers

The fireflies twinkled like stars on the ground,
As frogs played guitar, making quite the sound.
A raccoon in shades sang a silly song,
While dancing around, where he felt he belonged.

The night wore a blanket, warm and so bright,
With giggles and laughter echoing light.
A caterpillar strummed on a leaf-tuned lute,
Turning every moment into a hoot!

Tales Carved in Bark

On an ancient trunk, stories unfold,
Of chipmunks who dream of being bold.
A wise old owl with glasses so round,
Reads the tales of whose laughs are renowned.

A woodpecker knocks, keeping the beat,
With squirrels who gather, dancing their feat.
The moss tells whispers of days long past,
With each little chuckle, they speed by fast.

Serenade of the Swaying Trees

In the garden, trees do dance,
Leaves a-chatter, take a chance.
Swaying left, then swaying right,
Who needs rhythm when there's light?

Branches whisper silly jokes,
Tickling vines, forget the oaks.
A nut drops down, a squirrel sighs,
Nature's laugh under sunny skies.

Breezes Carrying Tales of Yore

Here comes the breeze with gossip quick,
Blowing secrets, just for kicks.
Did you hear what the daisies said?
Rumor has it, they're well-fed!

Dandelions laugh, making puffs,
While grasshoppers dance, oh so tough.
The old oak chuckles, branches wide,
While the shy shrubs hide, trying to bide.

Reflections in a Tranquil Glade

In the glade, the river flows,
Splashing tales that everyone knows.
But wait! A frog jumps in the way,
With a ribbit-start, it steals the play!

Mirror drops turn shiny and bright,
Dancing droplets in sheer delight.
The dragonflies make faces at the sun,
Their tiny antics—oh, what fun!

The Gentle Weaving of Nature's Voice

Nature weaves with threads of glee,
Spinning tales on every tree.
A bark-topped whistle floats on air,
Filling spaces with laughter rare.

A spider's web, a lacy shout,
Inviting bees to come about.
Each rustling leaf, a playful tease,
In this giggle-fest of trees!

Patterns of Life in Tangled Roots

In a garden of whispers, roots twist and twist,
A tale of mischief, with laughter amidst.
Crickets do break-dance on thistles in bloom,
While ants hold a circus in the shade of the gloom.

Silly dandelions wear crowns made of fluff,
Wiggling their petals, pretending they're tough.
A snail joins the party, his shell keeps it cool,
While frogs jump around to their own little school.

The Coloring of Shadows at Dusk

Shadows are painting with colors so bright,
A purple giraffe has taken to flight.
The sun's saying goodbye with a wink from the west,
While clouds dress in pink, like they're off to a fest.

A mouse wears a hat made of popcorn and cheese,
While crickets recite poetry, aiming to please.
The moon starts to giggle as stars join the show,
Spreading sparkles of laughter, putting on quite the glow.

Lullabies Woven from Fragrant Air

Breezes hum softly, a sweet serenade,
As flowers play harp on the green forest glade.
A raccoon croons gently, with talent so rare,
While a hedgehog taps rhythm, without any care.

The night carries whispers, like secrets we share,
As fireflies twinkle, dancing without a care.
A chorus of crickets sings 'Don't go to bed!'
While the moon grins and listens, tipping his head.

A Dance of Light through Verdant Boughs

The trees wear their lanterns, all shimmering bright,
Hosting a ball where the shadows take flight.
Bunnies in bow ties line up for the dance,
While squirrels do a jig, oh, what a romance!

With twinkling leaves and an owl's gentle hoot,
They waltz through the night in their fanciest suit.
A fox spins around, showing off his fine tail,
As the stars giggle softly, telling their tale.

The Heartbeat of the Stream

The stream giggles as it flows,
Tickles the rocks where laughter grows.
Fish dance in the silvery spray,
Who knew water could light up the day?

A frog croaks jokes in the bright sun,
While turtles race, oh what fun!
Splashing about, they tell some tales,
Of silly ducks and windy gales.

Leaves whirl like dancers on a stage,
Nature's antics, every age.
Bubbles pop like tiny balloons,
While dragonflies hum merry tunes.

The current hums a silly song,
Who'd have thought a stream could throng?
With creatures that chat in chirpy blips,
Join in the fun, take a dip!

Secrets in the Untamed Roots

Beneath the trees, where shadows creep,
Secrets linger, promises keep.
Worms gossip about the latest trends,
While squirrels plot how to make amends.

The roots stretch out in a tangled spree,
A maze of laughter, wild and free.
Ants march proudly, in tidy rows,
With tiny hats and fancy clothes!

Mice gather for a midnight meal,
While owls hoot about the ideal steal.
Fungi giggle at each little jest,
In the kingdom of dirt, they're the best!

In this chaos, a tale unfolds,
Of daring adventures, legends bold.
Nature's carnival, strange and sweet,
With laughter echoing at every beat!

Murmurs Beneath the Surface

The pond whispers with bubbling glee,
Underneath, a world of spree.
Frogs are busy playing hide and seek,
While fish swim by, giving a cheeky peek.

Tadpoles chatter, 'What's the next play?'
In swirling eddies, they splash away.
Dragonflies flirt, showing off their grace,
With glittering wings in a wild race.

The reeds sway, sharing gossip bold,
Of little creatures, stories told.
Bubbles pop, laughter's sweet tune,
As turtles bask under the moon.

Here, beneath the shimmering crest,
Nature holds its comical fest.
Every ripple sings with cheer,
Join the fun; the laughter's near!

Veils of Green and Gold

Sunlight dances through leafy veils,
Where giggling spirits tell their tales.
The breeze tickles the branches high,
As butterflies twirl and dart by.

Hidden treasures in every nook,
A squirrel peeks from a storybook.
Chirps of birds, a lively rhyme,
Crafting joy, one beat at a time.

Glistening droplets like diamonds shine,
While nature plays at being divine.
A sneaky squirrel steals a nut,
And rolls away with a jolly strut.

Amidst the greens, let laughter unfold,
In the arms of nature, brave and bold.
Magic whispers in colors bright,
Embrace the joy, let spirits take flight!

Nature's Silent Confidant

In the park, a tree so grand,
It whispers secrets, unplanned.
Branches wave, a playful cheer,
While squirrels giggle, always near.

Leaves dance lightly to the ground,
A gentle rustle is the sound.
Birds stop by for a quick chat,
Discussing all that the world's at.

The Tangle of Branches and Dreams

A tiny bird begins to weave,
Through tangled limbs, it won't leave.
It builds a nest, a cozy spot,
For dreams of worms and sunny rot.

A twisty trunk with much to say,
Holds up the sky in a quirky way.
With blooms that smile and roots that yawn,
Who knew the fun could go till dawn?

Whispers of the Evening Dew

Dew drops gather, gleaming bright,
They giggle softly, pure delight.
Tickling leaves and grass below,
In the dark, they put on a show.

Each droplet shimmers, feels like jest,
The night's laughter puts dreams to rest.
But if you tiptoe close to hear,
They may just splash you, oh dear!

Wisdom Stored in Nature's Embrace

Old roots know all the silly tales,
Of river trips and fishy fails.
The bark holds whispers, secrets rare,
Of every creature that passed there.

Nature laughs in sunshine's glow,
With shadowy winks from below.
So sit a spell and hear the glee,
For wisdom lives in every tree.

The Poetry of Dappled Light

In the shade where sunlight plays,
Leaves flicker in a silly maze.
Squirrels dance with acorn glee,
While shadows tease the Bumblebee.

Giggling branches sway and bend,
They sing secrets that they send.
The ground below is soft and bright,
A perfect space for a bug's delight.

Ticklish breezes brush the ground,
With every gust, the joy abounds.
A sunbeam finds a cheeky spot,
Golden laughter, forget-me-not.

So come, dear friend, and take a seat,
In dappled light, we'll share a treat.
Nature's jesters, loud and clear,
Join the fun, and have no fear.

Arbor Dreams in Twilight's Touch

As twilight creeps on quiet feet,
The trees begin their playful beat.
Branches whisper, secrets share,
Like gossip queens without a care.

A curtsy here, a bow from there,
The trunks do twist in graceful flair.
Roots tap dance upon the earth,
Each leaf tells tales of their worth.

Owl hoots jokes from high above,
While fireflies wink with gleeful love.
The stars join in the merry scene,
And make the night a perfect dream.

So gather 'round, let laughter rise,
With every chuckle, reach the skies.
In the clasp of dusk's embrace,
Find the mirth in nature's grace.

Timeless Secrets of the Canopy

In the canopy, where chortles live,
Each branch are comedians ready to give.
The leaves, they snicker with flair and fun,
As sunlight pranks, and shadows run.

Mice in suits orchestrate a show,
While picky birds pick at missed info.
The winds carry laughter, a merry tune,
As squirrels trade tales by the light of the moon.

Secrets whispered in rustling tones,
The wise old trees share giggles and moans.
With acorns aplenty, the humor flows,
In this merry wood where mischief grows.

So come on in, hear the laughter sprout,
In nature's theater, there's never a drought.
Each moment a jest, a hilarious spree,
In the timeless secrets of the leafy spree.

Lush Verses of Life's Flow

In a glen where laughter sways,
Every flower has something to say.
With petals tickling the sunlight's face,
Time dances with a joyful grace.

The brook joins in with a bubbling joke,
While frogs hop high like they're on a smoke.
Butterflies flit with a cheeky grin,
Finding sweet nectar makes them spin.

Crickets chirp in rhythmic tone,
Their nighttime symphony well-known.
As stars wink down at the silliness,
Life flows on, full of giggly bliss.

So join the brawl of nature's jest,
In lush verses, find your quest.
With every chuckle, a seed is sown,
In the garden of joy, we've all grown.

Ballet of Branches Beneath the Sky

In the breeze they twist and sway,
Dancing branches hold their play.
Twirling leaves, a comical sight,
Ballet of nature, pure delight.

Squirrels join the lively spree,
Chasing shadows, zig and zag free.
A pirouette, then a tumble,
Nature's laughter makes us humble.

The sun peeks through in sheer surprise,
As branches wave, they seem to rise.
A crowd of clouds sees the show,
While nearby, a frog steals the glow.

Oh, how gleeful it all appears,
With nature's humor, we lose our fears.
Giggling winds, they shout, "Hooray!"
In this ballet, we want to stay.

Shadows of Stories Untold

In the twilight's gentle veil,
Shadows dance, a whispered tale.
Branches gossip, secrets spun,
With every breeze, a new pun.

Squirrels snicker, plotting schemes,
Chasing dreams in playful teams.
Branches wiggle, pulling pranks,
Making fun of leafy flanks.

Underneath the moonlight's beam,
Shadow puppets weave and scheme.
A tale of acorns, grand and bold,
That leave us all a little sold.

So gather round, let's share a laugh,
As shadows sketch a silly path.
With each giggle, let's unfold,
The jests of life, in shadows told.

The Lament of Fallen Leaves

Once so proud, they floated high,
Now they lie, a woeful sigh.
Rustling softly in the breeze,
Shares a joke 'tween roots and trees.

"Don't be sad!" a leaf did say,
"Life's a game, in a funny way!"
Rolling down the winding way,
They giggled at this grand ballet.

Golden crowns in heaps now rest,
Each a story, a tiny jest.
Summoned from their lofty perch,
They laugh together, in a church.

So raise a glass to greens gone bold,
And toast the tales these leaves have told.
For every fall brings joy anew,
In their script, we'll find our cue.

Beneath the Gnarled Embrace

In the arms of knotted grace,
Laughter echoes in this place.
Gnarled branches stretch, they hug tight,
Whispering jokes in the fading light.

A raccoon grins in the cool shade,
Plotting schemes with a leafy aid.
Branches tease, like old, dear friends,
Knowing laughter never ends.

Crickets chirp a playful tune,
As shadows grow beneath the moon.
The night unfolds with merry cheer,
Nature's whispers, oh so near.

So gather 'round, let merriment swell,
In the heart of the wood, there's magic to tell.
The gnarled embrace, a stage so grand,
Where humor dances, hand in hand.

Soft Songs of the Lulling Lake

A frog croaks with such flair,
It thinks it's quite a star!
The fish dance in the air,
While boats float on afar.

A dragonfly in a hat,
Pretends to be a bee.
A turtle wears a spat,
Sipping tea near a tree.

The reeds sway side to side,
In their own little groove.
The water can't decide,
If it's time to move.

A catfish reads a book,
On what fish ought to know.
While minnows take a look,
At the dance show below.

Nature's Ballet of Whispered Hopes

The leaves waltz in the breeze,
With giggles all around.
A squirrel climbs with ease,
While trying not to sound.

The daisies throw a fit,
When wind comes blowing by.
They sway and then they sit,
Like stars against the sky.

The bees hum silly tunes,
While butterflies parade.
In bloom beneath the moons,
The critters join the charade.

They celebrate the day,
With laughter loud and bright.
In nature's playful sway,
They dance until the night.

Beneath the Arc of Ancient Grace

Old trees tell tales so grand,
With twinkling eyes of green.
Their roots stretch out like hands,
Hiding secrets unseen.

A raccoon steals a snack,
Wearing stripes with great pride.
He looks to make a pact,
With squirrels by his side.

The branches form a stage,
For owls to hoot and play.
Their wisdom cannot age,
As night turns into day.

The shadows leap and prance,
In a funny little jig.
While stars begin to dance,
And the crickets start to gig.

Tresses of Time and Memory

A vine wraps round a gate,
In a tangle of delight.
It sways and seems to skate,
Underneath the moonlight.

The daisies wear a crown,
Of forget-me-nots so blue.
While peeking upside down,
A worm joins in the view.

The petals laugh and giggle,
As the wind spins 'round and 'round.
With every twist and wiggle,
They spread joy to the ground.

With each soft, gentle breeze,
Time dances in a whirl.
In nature's joyful tease,
Every leaf becomes a twirl.

Whispers of the Lingering Breeze

In the garden where giggles play,
Leaves dance about in a cheeky way.
A tickle from nature, oh so spry,
As squirrels plot mischief beneath the sky.

Breezes tease with a playful touch,
Swirling around without a rush.
Flowers giggle, the daisies sway,
An ensemble of joy in bright array.

Even the grass has a laugh or two,
Making funny faces, what a view!
Whispers soft, as the sun goes down,
A ticklish breeze make the flowers frown.

So next time you stroll by the trees,
Listen closely, hear the glee.
Nature's humor is all around,
In every rustle, a giggle found.

The Silhouette of Sighs

Under twilight's playful gaze,
Shadows stretch in quirky ways.
Shapes and forms begin to prance,
A comical, twilight dance.

Sighs escape from the evening's chill,
As owls wonder, 'What's the thrill?'
Branches sway like they've had too much,
A flurry of laughter in nature's touch.

Laughter echoes through the trees,
Silly secrets sway on the breeze.
The moon grins wide, in the night so bright,
While stars chuckle in sheer delight.

What a sight, this funny show,
Nature's antics put on a glow.
Beneath the stars we find our fun,
In the silhouette, we play and run.

Beneath the Shadowed Canopy

Underneath where secrets blend,
Leaves chatter like the best of friends.
Jokes are told in rustling tones,
Even the ground joins with its stones.

A raccoon rolls in a jester's hat,
While squirrels giggle and have a spat.
The branches wave like a clown's big shoes,
Carrying laughter in all its hues.

Pinecones drop with comical thuds,
Creating a symphony of friendly jugs.
The canopy sways to an offbeat tune,
As shadows twist in a lively swoon.

Come join the whimsy, take a peek,
Nature's humor is never bleak.
Beneath the canopy, let laughter thrive,
In this silly world, we come alive.

Echoes of the Waving Branches

Branches wave like they've had too much,
Bowing and nodding with a gentle touch.
Whispers echo in a playful twist,
On this funny rollicking list.

Birds chirp jokes in the morning light,
As butterflies giggle, taking flight.
The wind joins in with a hurried whoosh,
Creating a soundtrack for a jolly push.

In every rustle, a story to tell,
Nature spins tales as it ring the bell.
Funny antics flutter through the air,
A comedy show without a care.

So listen closely to the trees,
They put on shows, the staff of glee.
In the echoes, find your cheer,
Laughter reigns, come gather near.

Songs of the Swaying Knots

In the grove where giggles bloom,
Trees dance like they're in a room.
Branches twist in playful fiends,
Whispering secrets, bending dreams.

Bugs sing tunes on sticky webs,
While squirrels wobble, making ebbs.
Caught in knots, they swing and sway,
Nature's jesters come out to play.

Leaves chuckle as the breezes tease,
Rabbits hop like they've had cheese.
Beneath the branches, laughter sings,
In this place where mischief springs.

So join the rascals, don't be late,
In this grove, we celebrate.
With every turn and twist we take,
Dance with joy, for laughter's sake.

Reflection in the Water's Eye

Puddles wink with mirrored grins,
Creating ripples where fun begins.
Frogs perform a splashy show,
As dragonflies say, "Look at me go!"

The trees lean in to catch a peek,
"Who's the fairest?" they all squeak.
Bobbing ducks quack with delight,
In this dance of day and night.

The sun drops in with a cheesy smile,
Water laughs, "Stay for a while!"
Happy fish wiggle in surprise,
Playing tag beneath blue skies.

When twilight falls, the world will rest,
Yet the pond bubbles, quite the jest.
With every ripple, glee expands,
Join the frolic of water bands!

Harmony of the Stirring Leaves

The leaves gossip in breezy tones,
Swapping stories in hushed groans.
A tap-tap here, a rustle there,
Nature's band, a lively fair.

With every breeze, a new tale spins,
A leaf drops down; the mischief begins.
"Catch me if you can!" it dares,
As autumn curls with tousled hairs.

The branches shake in fits of glee,
"Who can sway the wildest, me?"
Spin and twirl, a leafy waltz,
With every flap, forget your faults.

As shadows dance and evenings fall,
Under the stars, we hear their call.
Join in harmony, leave your cares,
With the stirring leaves, laughter shares!

Lullabies to the Wandering Souls

In twilight's glow, the world unravels,
With giggles echoing on moonlit travels.
Stars wink down, their twinkling jokes,
While shadows play with silly folks.

A gentle breeze hums soft and low,
"Close your eyes, let the laughter flow."
The night sings sweet, like tickles around,
As sleepy smiles in dreams are found.

Gnomes and fairies, on the roam,
Whisper lullabies that feel like home.
Rest your head, let the fun unfold,
In a world of wonders yet untold.

So wanderers, embrace the night,
With dreams that tickle, pure delight.
In this realm where giggles swirl,
Sleep tight, dear souls, give joy a twirl!

Illuminate the Gloomy Passages

In shadows where whispers play,
A lamp knocked over, went astray.
The ghosts of jokes float in the air,
As giggles tumble down the stair.

A cat in boots begins to prance,
Knocking over chairs, oh what a dance!
With every swish of a tail, we grin,
As echoes of laughter bounce within.

Glorious beams cut through the dark,
As quirks of light ignite a spark.
We stumble on truths wrapped in jest,
Where gloom retreats and smiles are blessed.

So gather 'round, it's time to glow,
With tales that ripple, ebb and flow.
We'll light up paths where shadows trod,
Bringing joy to every little nod.

The Lengthening Gaze of Ancient Trees

With roots that stretch and limbs that wave,
The wise old trees begin to rave.
They share their thoughts in rustling tones,
Of squirrels, acorns, and ancient phones.

Their bark, a canvas, tells a tale,
Of lovers lost and cats that wail.
In evening light, their shadows tease,
Creating shapes that tickle knees.

When wind picks up, they sway and creak,
A jubilant dance, their voices peak.
In laughter shared, they sway along,
To nature's rhythm, a joyful song.

So take a glance at these majestic sights,
Where humor blooms and joy ignites.
For in their gaze, absurdity thrives,
And timeless chuckles still survive.

Whispers Beneath the Boughs

Beneath the branches, we convene,
Where secrets linger, bright and keen.
A chorus of giggles floats so near,
As silly notions come to cheer.

The boughs above play peek-a-boo,
With shadows that dance in all they do.
They gossip low about the moon,
And tell of socks lost way too soon.

With every breeze, a chuckle springs,
Nature's own gag, the joy it brings.
In every rustle, a tale replays,
Of prankster spirits in playful ways.

So gather 'round and lean in tight,
For laughter grows beneath the light.
In whispers soft, life's joys abound,
Where silliness and peace are found.

Elegy of the Swaying Silhouette

The figures dance in twilight's glow,
With shadows casting tales we know.
A jester's cap and floppy shoes,
As silliness sprouts from every muse.

They bend and twist, the night a stage,
A playful script at every age.
With laughter spilling from their seams,
As twilight winks and softly beams.

Each curve and sway, a giggle tossed,
In every movement, no laughter lost.
They prance and leap, the scene unfolds,
A tribute to fun as night beholds.

So raise a glass to silhouettes,
Who sway and jive, no regrets.
In moonlit grace, they find their place,
With every chuckle, they embrace.

Secrets Danced in Twilight

In the dusk, the shadows play,
Whispers zooming, come what may.
Trees giggle softly beneath their breath,
Tales of mischief, life and death.

A squirrel dons a tiny hat,
Thinks he's grand, just like a cat.
The moon's a grape, the stars are cheese,
Life's a feast, if you please.

Fireflies skip in tangled lines,
Swapping jokes as sunlight shines.
Each flicker spins a little jest,
Dancing secrets, never rest.

Twilight winks, the world's a clown,
Throw confetti, upside down!
In twilight's glow, laughter swells,
With each heartbeat, magic dwells.

The Language of the Shaded Glade

In the glade where shadows tease,
Frogs croak jokes with perfect ease.
A chubby rabbit, crown on head,
Declares the day, 'No time for bed!'

Leaves whisper tales of grasshopper dreams,
While crickets plot in silver beams.
A snail recites a love-sick tune,
Trying hard to woo the moon.

Among the ferns, laughter grows,
Twirling round like autumn's prose.
Mice with mustaches, oh what a sight,
Dancing twirls till the morning light.

The sun dips low, colors collide,
Nature chuckles, can't help but guide.
In each rustle, a giggle hides,
As the shaded glade abides.

Withering Dreams in the Dusk

As the sun bows down to sleep,
The night steals dreams from shadows deep.
A sleepy owl, with droopy eyes,
Spouts off riddles, oh such lies!

The stars tumble like clumsy teens,
Tripping through the sky, oh what scenes!
Imaginary creatures with soft, wild hair,
Playing hopscotch in mid-air.

Under the moon, dreams mingle tight,
Whispers of giggles in the night.
Each thought a jester, flipping pranks,
As reason tumbles, lost in ranks.

Withering dreams may fade away,
But laughter lingers, here to stay.
As dusk unfolds its wrapping dance,
Life wears a crown, given the chance.

Stories Written in the Rustling Breeze

The wind tells tales, oh so spry,
Of rabbits that laugh and owls that fly.
A gentle nudge, a playful tease,
As stories travel on the breeze.

Whispers weave through branches high,
Tickling leaves as they float by.
Squirrels argue over acorn bets,
While the moon feels like regret.

Winds of fortune, secrets bloom,
In every whiff, there's room to zoom.
Breezy gossip, truth unspun,
Life in motion, all in fun.

When the day draws to a close,
And laughter in the twilight grows,
Listen close, the world will tease,
For stories ride on the rustling breeze.

The Grace of Nature's Quiet Harmonics

In the shade of leafy arms,
Nature hums her silly charms.
Bugs dance to a buzzing tune,
While frogs croak under a bright moon.

Swaying trees lose their cool,
As squirrels play a silly fool.
Their acorn stash all in disarray,
They complain, 'We'll get it back one day!'

Breezes tease with feathered sighs,
Twirling leaves in merry highs.
Nature laughs with a mischievous wink,
'Life's a thrill, don't you think?'

In this world of nature's jest,
Every branch is a curious quest.
With every rustle and giggle here,
Nature is the jester we all cheer.

Lost in the Labyrinth of Branches

I wandered through the leafy maze,
Lost in thoughts, in nature's gaze.
Then came a branch that waved hello,
And whispered secrets I didn't know.

A squirrel turned to play the guide,
With a nut it offered in proud stride.
'Follow me, we'll find a treat!'
But all it led me to was 'tweet!'

Branches speak in tangled rhyme,
Swaying softly, they pass the time.
Each path leads to a giggly spot,
Where nature laughs and time is caught.

In the labyrinth, I twist and twirl,
Branches giggle as they unfurl.
'You're stuck with us, so have a ball!'
Laughter echoes, 'Just heed the call!'

A Symphony of Leaves in the Wind

Leaves in the breeze hold a tune,
Whispering secrets and silly swoon.
They twirl and spin, a dance so grand,
Nature conducts with a playful hand.

Each rustle adds to the friendly song,
A melody where all belong.
Birds join in with chirps and tweets,
Creating harmony, feel the beats!

A leaf joked, 'I'm off to fly!'
It swirled away as if to try.
Another teased, 'Come chase me, friend!'
Nature's music seems to never end.

In this symphony, don't be aloof,
Join the dance beneath the roof.
Nature's laughter echoes, deep and kind,
A cheerful tune for us to find.

Reveries Caught in Tangled Tendrils

Tendrils twist with glee and mirth,
Caught in dreams of playful Earth.
They stretch and curl in the afternoon,
Singing softly a little tune.

A vine smirked, 'I'll pull you tight,'
But only pulled me into light.
I tumbled down in fits of giggles,
Nature's trick, oh how it wiggles!

Tangled branches tease the eye,
Catching thoughts like clouds that fly.
As shadows dance in the golden glow,
I laughed and spun, 'Take that, you crow!'

In the whispers of nature's blend,
Reveries shape, though they may bend.
With each tangle, a tale unfurls,
Nature's yarn spins smiles in swirls.

Reverie in a Fragile Dance

In the breeze, the branches twirl,
Leaves giggle as they swirl.
A squirrel performs a silly feat,
While birds join in, oh what a treat!

Dancing shadows play on the ground,
Tickling toes that skip around.
The wind whispers jokes in delight,
As nature's laughter takes flight.

A wobbly rabbit hops nearby,
Trip and tumble, oh my, oh my!
With carefree jumps, it steals the scene,
In this garden, life is a dream.

Beneath a sky, so bright and blue,
We laugh at clouds that drift askew.
In this fragile, joyful get-together,
Every little mishap's light as a feather.

Chasing Sunlight Through the Leaves

Sunbeams peek through every twig,
Dancing with shadows, doing a jig.
With giggles, the children run and spin,
Capturing warmth, oh, where to begin?

A monkey grins from a leafy throne,
Yelling, "Come join, you're not alone!"
Swinging high on branches bright,
They leap about, what a silly sight!

In the rustling grass, they hide and seek,
The trees chuckle as they peek.
A rogue butterfly flutters by,
Tickling noses, oh my, oh my!

They chase after time, but it's still a game,
Playing tag, no cares, no shame.
In this arena of light and cheer,
Laughter echoes, and joy draws near.

Harvesting Dreams in the Green Shade

In the meadow where whispers play,
Dreams are plucked in a quirky way.
Buggies dash and chase the breeze,
While laughter ripples through the trees.

Sunset hues, a tapestry bright,
Amidst the giggles, oh what a sight!
Upside-down, the flowers bloom,
Like hats worn by a silly cartoon.

Bouncing thoughts float like balloons,
Cartwheeling rabbits in playful tunes.
Jars filled with giggles, oh, what a catch,
Harvesting grins, a delightful match.

Under the canopy, secrets unfold,
With each story, a joke retold.
In this playful patch of shared delight,
Every heartbeat echoes through the night.

Incantations Among the Rooted Dreams

In the shadows where wise roots lie,
Whispers tickle, and balloons fly high.
A gnome with a grin spins tales anew,
Of mischief and fun, all bright and true.

Mushrooms dance in their polka-dot suits,
Giggling along with their fuzzy boots.
The fairies sprinkle humor like rain,
As laughter erupts in joyful refrain.

Tracing stories on the gentle ground,
With sketches drawn all around.
Creatures tap-dance in the moonlit gleam,
Spellbound in this whimsical dream.

Among the trees, we twirl and prance,
In this magical, rib-tickling dance.
With every step, a chuckle escapes,
Rooted in fun, no need for capes.

Flowing Thoughts Beneath the Arch

Beneath the arch where whispers play,
Thoughts drift like leaves on a sunny day.
Swaying gently, a laughter's tune,
Tickling the air like a jovial rune.

Yet a squirrel thinks it's all a jest,
Wearing acorns like a furry vest.
He dances with glee, a tiny brigade,
While the wise old tree keeps its shade.

Butterflies giggle, they flutter and glide,
Chasing each other, a colorful ride.
Who knew a breeze could cause such delight?
As whispers plot mischief from morning to night.

But beware the breeze, oh winds of fate,
For it might just turn your hat to a plate!
With laughter abounding and shadows that tease,
Life's funnier side lives among the trees.

The Tapestry of Time and Shade

In the tapestry twinkling with laughter,
Time weaves stories, but what comes after?
Each shadow's a prankster, hiding and seeking,
Making time twist in giggles, not freaking!

A tickle of sunlight, a playful breeze,
Paints the world in glorious ease.
Leaves whisper jokes in a rustling tune,
Making even the grumpiest laugh like a loon.

Underneath branches, giddy tales bloom,
Where moss has decided to form a lounge room.
And critters, with flair, put on a grand show,
Turning the simple into a vibrant tableau!

So wander through fabric of shade and chat,
Find the humor in moments, imagine that!
For life's just a jest with a punchline ahead,
Where laughter blooms, no worries to dread.

Breath of the Earthbound Spirits

In the breath of greens where spirits reside,
They chuckle and giggle, with secrets to bide.
Dancing on roots, with mischievous flair,
Poking fun at the clouds floating unaware.

Their laughter cascades like ripples on ponds,
Where frogs join the chorus and sing silly songs.
Each quirk and twist of the wind is a whiff,
Of humor brewed fresh from an earthly sift.

The grass teases toes, a ticklish affair,
As squirrels throw shade in their raucous lair.
Foliage chuckles, it rustles with glee,
Creating a laughter that's wild and free!

So take a deep breath, feel the earth's smiles,
In this playful realm, humor stretches for miles.
For spirits abound, in giggles they blend,
Making the mundane a magical trend.

Hidden Routes of the Heart

In hidden paths where giggles reside,
The heart takes a turn, with joy as its guide.
Every twist and turn, a whimsical race,
Promises laughter, wrapped in soft grace.

Past shadows of boulders that whisper in glee,
Gnomes plot their riddles beneath the old tree.
Moss carpets the trails where secrets are spun,
Each heartbeat a drum, in the warmth of the sun.

Every step holds a mystery, light as a breeze,
Tickling one's soul, planting laughter with ease.
And the flowers parade in colors so bright,
Opening hearts to embrace the delight.

So wander these routes, let humor unfurl,
For in every corner, life's quirks swirl.
Hidden delights in each glance and each start,
Become the joy, the routes of the heart.

Tides of Time Beneath the Canopy

A tree with a grin, sways with delight,
Its leaves whisper jokes in the warm light.
The squirrels throw acorns, hoping for laughs,
While birds crack the code of their funny gaffes.

The branches are arms that tickle the skies,
As shadows dance softly, no need for disguise.
The breeze plays a tune, a whimsical song,
With every light flutter, nothing feels wrong.

The roots tell a tale, of days gone by,
When giggles grew loud and spirits flew high.
A trophy of laughter, they hold every cheer,
As life swings by softly, with nothing to fear.

So gather 'round friends, take a seat and unwind,
Leave worries behind, let fun be your mind.
In the shade of this giant, where silliness blooms,
We toast to the laughter that fills all our rooms.

Reflections on a Gentle Stream

A babble of giggles, flows down the path,
With ripples that dance, inspiring a laugh.
Frogs leap in rhythm, to nature's own beat,
As minnows start a conga, oh, ain't life sweet!

The rocks wear a grin, slick and so smooth,
They chuckle and chuckle, with every groove.
A dragonfly darts, in a dazzling flair,
While fish tell tall tales of voyages rare.

The sun casts a wink, through branches up high,
Painting a backdrop for humor to fly.
With each little splash, a giggle ignites,
As laughter merges with the sparkling lights.

So dip in your toes, let joy be the theme,
Float down the current, and savor the dream.
With nature as witness, the world seems so grand,
In this playful oasis, together we stand.

Dreaming in the Shade of Ancients

Beneath towering giants, where shadows entwine,
The caress of their wisdom feels simply divine.
A seat on the grass, with a view of the past,
Where roots cradle secrets, oh how they last!

The gnarled old branches weave tales of delight,
Of squirrels who plotted the best acorn heist.
With leaves that are clapping, and roots that incite,
The air fills with chuckles, oh what a sight!

A picnic of laughter, all spread on the ground,
As ants join the feast, with a marching sound.
With whispers of breezes, and rustles of fun,
We dance with the shadows, till the day is done.

So gaze at the heavens, and dream out your schemes,
Let the ancients around you fulfill all your dreams.
In this joyous embrace, where magic ignites,
Every moment we dwell, is a heart filled with light.

The Comfort of Green Embrace

In a cloak of green, where the goofiness thrives,
Every blade of grass tells wild jokes that connive.
The flowers wear smiles, in colors so bright,
While butterflies giggle on this joyful sight.

With vines that are ticklish, wrapping up tight,
Nature spins stories, both silly and light.
The sun plays peek-a-boo, as shadows retreat,
In this haven of glee, let's dance to the beat.

A ukulele's strumming, invites us to sing,
While wiggles and wobbles become all the thing.
The peace here is cozy, like a wrapped-up hug,
In this world of keen laughter, we all feel the tug.

So come take a rest under layers of glee,
Leave worries behind, let your spirit run free.
With a grin and a chuckle, life feels so grand,
In the arms of this nature, we make our own band.

The Poetry of Patience Unfolds

In the garden, still I wait,
For a quirk, for a twist of fate.
The flowers giggle, roots do chuckle,
As I ponder, in this green huddle.

Daisies tease the sun up high,
While tulips play peek-a-boo, oh my!
I pat my knees, what a silly sight,
Nature laughs from morning to night.

Bumblebees buzz, dance a jig,
In the air, they zoom, so big!
While I sip tea, with a grin so wide,
Waiting for blooms, with mischief they hide.

So here I linger, just having fun,
In the shade of leaves, under the sun.
The poetry of patience, oh what a tease,
As I chuckle with ants, amidst the trees.

Embracing the Earthly Whispers

The earth hums softly, a silly song,
Where squirrels scamper, nothing feels wrong.
In the dirt, worms wriggle with glee,
Laughing at humans, just look and see!

Crickets chirp jokes, with timing just right,
As the moonlight dances, it's quite a sight.
Frogs croak verses, oh such a hoot,
Each ribbit an echo, in their green suit.

Mice hold a conference, planning a feast,
While grease stains dance with a buttered beast.
Nature chuckles, its laughter profound,
In the whispers of earth, joy's all around.

So listen closely to what they're saying,
The absurdity of life, that's playing!
With every rustle, embrace the cheer,
In this wild world, humor's always near.

Messages in Falling Petals

Petals drift down like goofy notes,
As trees send messages, through swoops and floats.
Each swirl a secret, a giggle, a grin,
Telling stories of chaos, where fun begins.

A ladybug laughs, dressed in red,
As petals whisper, 'Off with your head!'
But she just rolls, on her tiny back,
Giving the flowers a laugh attack.

Winds carry tales from branches above,
Of clumsy squirrels and ungrateful doves.
Each chuckle in the breeze is a cue,
To enjoy life's bloopers, in flowered hue.

So when petals fall and lands are bright,
Join the laughter, with pure delight.
For in these moments, joy's sure to swell,
In the dance of petals, we find stories to tell.

Shadows of Stories Yet Untold

In shadowed corners, secrets loom,
With critters plotting their next big boom.
Each rustle brings laughter, a wink, a tease,
As they gather 'round like old friends with ease.

A cat slinks by with a knowing smirk,
As shadows giggle, it's quite the perk.
Mice share cheese dreams of daring escapes,
While bats tell tales of nighttime scrapes.

From tree to tree, whispers in flight,
Of grand adventures, what a delight!
Glimmers of moonlight make mischief arise,
As shadows take shape and surprise our eyes.

So dance in the gloom, let stories unfold,
In the laughter of shadows, be brave, be bold.
For within every shadow lies a jesting soul,
Waiting for laughter to take full control.

Lament of the Gentle Breeze

Oh gentle breeze, you play so sly,
You ruffle my hair as you rush by.
You tickle my nose with a quiet whoosh,
Then laugh as I sneeze with a violent push.

You tease the flowers, dance on leaves,
Spinning a tale that nobody believes.
Do you know you're the cause of my flail?
Darting like a fish, I'm losing my trail.

Under the sun, you glide with grace,
While I trip over roots, what a disgrace!
You whisper sweet nothings, I laugh in glee,
Just don't tangle me up in your spree!

So carry on with your gusty glee,
But don't make a fool out of poor me.
With every swirl, my sanity wobbles,
Oh, the laughter from such silly troubles!

Serenity in the Shade

In the cool embrace of a leafy hide,
Where mischief winkles and giggles reside.
A tiny bug, on a branch swings low,
Who thought a nap would steal the show?

The squirrels plot pranks in the afternoon light,
Stealing my snacks, oh, what a sight!
While I sip my drink in this tranquil nook,
They're plotting and scheming, can't they just cook?

The shadows dance as the sun rolls away,
Tickling the ground with a bright ballet.
I chuckle as nature plays its tune,
With critters cavorting, from morn until noon.

So here I'll lounge, with laughter so near,
Amidst the antics that bring me cheer.
The shade wraps around, a gentle embrace,
In this silly haven, I've found my place!

Cascading Thoughts of Nature

Thoughts tumble down like a babbling brook,
Swirling and dancing in every nook.
The trees snicker softly, wrapping around,
With whispers of laughter that echo the ground.

Chipmunks exchange the juiciest tales,
Of sunburnt nuts and forgotten snails.
While bunnies debate who hops with more flair,
In the ruckus of nature, who really cares?

Each leaf is a giggle, each branch is a pun,
While daisies giggle under the sun.
In nature's own comedy, I find my muse,
With all these antics, I cannot refuse.

So let them prattle, let the laughter roll,
For in this ecosystem, I've found my role.
With whimsy and joy, life's a grand play,
In cascading thoughts that brighten the day!

The Language of Swaying Limbs

In the language of limbs, the trees sway and chat,
With each gentle flick, they share a small spat.
"Oh, your branch is drooping!" a neighbor will tease,
As they rebuff with a rustle, like leaves in the breeze.

The trunks spread gossip like old friends would do,
"Have you seen that new bush? Oh, it's quite the view!"
Beneath the green canopy, chuckles ignite,
As squirrels roll back with a flourish just right.

Some branches intertwine as they dance with ease,
Creating a festival, swaying in peace.
With roots intertwined, they weave tales so lame,
Yet every soft chuckle feels just like a game.

So here in the forest, we laugh and play,
In the joy of our language, come join our fray.
With each gentle sway, we share in our fun,
In the comedy of nature, we're all number one!

The Breath of Ancients in Every Leaf

In a forest of giggles, the trees have a laugh,
They whisper old secrets like a nature math.
Frogs in tuxedos, dancing in the rain,
Each leaf is a story, no thought is in vain.

The squirrels are jesters with acorns to toss,
They poke fun at the shadows, the line's not a loss.
Branches play tag with the clouds up above,
Rustling in rhythm, they twirl like a dove.

Nature beams brightly, with a wink and a swirl,
As flowers giggle softly, they dance and they twirl.
The breeze carries jokes that tickle the ground,
Laughter and wonder in each moment found.

A symphony of chuckles, all nature's big show,
Leaves burst with charm, putting on quite a glow.
Let's gather the giggles, share secrets at dusk,
In this leafy abode where the playful don't rust.

Chronicles Written in Bark and Sky

Trees hold the stories; they're inked in their bark,
A diary of giggles, bright stamps in the dark.
Each knot tells a tall tale, fantastically spun,
As the wind swirls around, oh what a pun!

Branches become pages open wide to reveal,
The antics of critters that twirl and squeal.
Clouds doodle in gray, then bloom into white,
As sunbeams conspire to tickle our sight.

Squirrels write poems with acorns and rhyme,
While raccoons compose ballads that shimmer with time.
Breezes are whispers of stories retold,
In this zany archive, the laughter is bold.

Together we chuckle, our laughter takes flight,
In a chronicle blooming under starlit night.
The sky joins the chorus, it never backs down,
As trees sway with glee, wearing laughter's own crown.

The Gentle Comfort of Sunny Corners

In the warm little nook where the sunlight would spill,
Mice play the accordions, light footed, and shrill.
Basking in laughter, they catch easy rays,
While daisies gossip in dainty displays.

With tea leaves and giggles, the breezes rise high,
As butterflies flutter, they sip most awry.
Ants march in rhythm with little top hats,
Making a fuss over crumbs and free snacks!

The corner becomes magic, where humor unfolds,
Sunbeams weaving laughter like stories retold.
Rabbits break dance on a patch of soft moss,
Their floppy-eared style is a total win-loss!

In these sunny delights, the world feels brand new,
Chasing away worries, as laughter breaks through.
With giggles and warmth, we cherish this space,
In corners of sunshine, we dance with pure grace.

Nature's Whisper in the Stillness

In the hush of the forest, where silence sings loud,
The trees crack a joke, and the mushrooms feel proud.
Each shadow is painted with tickles and glee,
In stillness, we find the humor that's free.

Moss cushions the earth with its velvety laugh,
Inviting us closer to the silly staff.
The stream gurgles softly, like whispers of fun,
Tickling the toes of each creature that runs.

A pause brings the giggles that echo through time,
As the petals converse, each one full of rhyme.
In the quiet of nature, the laughter takes flight,
Creating a symphony that sparkles the night.

Amongst the still wonders, we join in the jest,
Living in moments where nature's the best.
In laughs that are hidden, we seek and we share,
Finding joy in the stillness, with love everywhere.

Sighs of the Swaying Trunk

Beneath a tree with a twisty grin,
The branches dance, let the laughter begin.
They tickle the sky, a comedic show,
Spinning tales of breezes, they steal the glow.

A squirrel winks with a nutty plan,
As birds scoop down, they form a band.
With chirps that echo like jokes in the air,
The trunk shakes lightly, a laugh to share.

Oh, how the leaves break into a spin,
"Which way is up?" they ask with a grin.
The sunlight hops like a playful pup,
And shadows join in, never giving up.

As dusk rolls in, the giggles flow,
The trunk leans back, stealing the show.
With a heart so light, it sways and swirls,
In this tree of chuckles, let joy unfurl.

Echoes of Serenity's Embrace

In a park where whispers tickle the ground,
The leaves gossip secrets, oh what a sound!
A breeze plays tricks with hair and hats,
While ducks quack loudly, sharing their chats.

The branches swing low with a playful tease,
"Who wants to dance? Come move with the breeze!"
With every rustle, the laughter multiplies,
As shadows step out, sporting surprise ties.

"Catch me if you can," the sunlight beams,
As butterflies flutter, weaving bright dreams.
Hiccups of joy, a babbling brook,
Echoes of fun, take a second look.

As day slips away, the fun's not done,
The stars giggle softly, one by one.
In the arms of the night, with a wink and a race,
Serenity chuckles, each glance a warm embrace.

Fragments of an Afternoon Reverie

On a lazy afternoon, with clouds drifting slow,
A bee's on a mission, wings all aglow.
"Excuse me, dear flower, I've come for a drink!
Your nectar's the best! What do you think?"

A spider spins webs with intricate flair,
"It's a work of art, if you stop and stare!"
And ants march proudly in a straight, silly line,
"Box lunch in tow, we're feeling just fine!"

The sun tickles petals with a warm, golden glow,
While shadows below put on a grand show.
"Copycat clouds!" they whisper with glee,
"Let's play dress-up, me and thee!"

As laughter surrounds, in this whimsical space,
Time dances lightly, a cheeky embrace.
Fragments of joy in this carefree ballet,
An afternoon's dream that just wants to stay.

Cradle of Affection in Leafy Halls

Nestled in greenery, a playground unfolds,
Where branches wave gently, in stories retold.
"Join us," they beckon, "for a romp under trees,
We've got jokes and laughter, come swing with the breeze!"

In leafy confines, the petals all cheer,
As critters and critters share giggles sincere.
The wind joins the fun, whistling bright tunes,
Inviting the flowers to dance with the moons.

A couple meets there, on a bench made of bark,
With smirks and soft whispers that dance in the dark.
"Is it me or the tree that's blushing today?"
And the branches just giggle, come out to play.

As twilight blankets the cradle with love,
The stars twinkle brightly, like winks from above.
In the leafy embrace where affection stands tall,
A heartfelt chuckle whispers, "You're welcome, all!"

Murmurs of the Wind's Embrace

The breeze tickles trees with a giggle,
As branches sway and twist to wiggle.
Leaves whisper secrets, oh so silly,
While branches sway, the squirrels get frilly.

The sun beams down with a playful glow,
Playing tag with shadows down below.
Frolicsome branches do their own thing,
While birds tweet jokes, oh how they sing!

Caught in the rustle of the funnier side,
Where each gust of wind has nowhere to hide.
Nature's own stage with the wildest glee,
Where laughter floats free, just like a bee!

So next time you hear a soft, breezy sound,
Know it's just nature's jest going round.
Join in the laughter, let yourself sway,
This playful dance is what brightens the day!

Echoes in Shades of Green

In hues of green, the laughter is loud,
Where leafy figures gather a crowd.
They whisper jokes that tickle the roots,
Even the flowers sport silly boots!

Amongst the ferns, laughter bounces,
Mischievous chipmunks hop in pounces.
Each shade of green with a tale to spin,
A comedy show where the fun begins!

Caterpillars rolling, what a display,
They giggle and wiggle the afternoon away.
Amidst all the humor, a snail takes a bow,
He's slow to respond, but we love him somehow!

So stroll through the greens, let laughter flow,
Find joy in the tiny, let your worries go.
For in every corner, amidst the serene,
Lies a world of echoes, so funny, so green!

The Graceful Dance of Shadows

In the soft daylight, shadows start to prance,
Each one a dancer, oh what a chance!
They twirl and they leap, in merry delight,
Flirting with sunlight, oh what a sight!

As evening approaches, they grow long and lean,
A tug-of-war game, oh what a routine!
They creep and they crawl, just trying to play,
While old oaks chuckle, "Come join the ballet!"

One shadow trips over a stick on the ground,
Yet still it recovers, with grace it's renowned.
Here comes a breeze, swirling, giggling near,
"What's graceful? Just shadows, or laughter we hear?"

So dance with your shadows, let giggles entwine,
For under the sun, there's no need to confine.
Laughter and shadows best friends, a team,
Just follow their steps, and join in the dream!

Secrets Held in Leafy Dreams

In dreams of leaves, giggles unfold,
Beneath the boughs, secrets retold.
A leaf on the breeze whispers, "What fun!"
While rustling branches whisper, "Run, run, run!"

Each leaf has a tale, oh so absurd,
From mischievous crickets to a wordless bird.
"Why did the twig bend? It wanted a hug!"
Thus laughter erupts from the forest bug!

A butterfly flutters in wobbly air,
It giggles and flutters without a care.
Twisting and whirling in sunshine so bright,
Each flutter is joy, a comedic delight!

So remember the secrets that shade can provide,
Where laughter and dreams intertwine side by side.
In leafy dreams, let your spirit ignite,
For joy is a treasure that dances in light!

The Silence of Autumn's Caress

In the breeze, leaves dance and spin,
Cackling squirrels, plotting a win.
Chasing shadows, oh how they prance,
Nature's stage where they take a chance.

Pumpkin smiles on every street,
Autumn's share of truth or treat.
Goblins giggle, spooky delight,
At nightfall, they take to flight.

With every crunch beneath my shoe,
The trees whisper secrets, just a few.
But don't ask them, they're tight-lipped,
These crafty branches, all equipped.

Yet in these woods, laughter's a wave,
Echoing tales of those who misbehave.
So here I roam, with a grin on my face,
Among the cackles of nature's embrace.

Tethered by Nature's Roots

Rabbits hop and tease the crows,
In tangled thickets, where mischief grows.
Gnarled branches twist and twine,
Giggles emerge, all by design.

The sun peeks through, a cheeky sprite,
As ants march in parties, what a sight!
They steal the crumbs while the birds do glare,
Oh! Nature's circus, with quite the flair.

Tangled in vines, a feline waits,
Plotting escape from the gopher's gates.
He stretches wide, let the games ensue,
A pounce and a roll, the chase in view.

Yet even as I chuckle and trot,
I wonder what tales these roots have got.
Their whispers sway with each gentle breeze,
Funny how they tease with such simple ease.

The Reverie of a Sunlit Glen

In the glen where daisies play,
Dancing under the sun's warm ray.
Butterflies flit, painting the air,
Each one giggles without a care.

A squirrel juggles acorns with glee,
While bees buzz by, 'Oh look at me!'
Nature's carnival, wild and free,
A trunk spins tales, sip tea with me.

The grass is soft as a featherbed,
Where rabbits sigh and lay their heads.
A lofty tree, it crafts a show,
Because treetops know how to let go.

So as the day dims and crickets sing,
The glen erupts into spring's own fling.
With laughter and joy, it's never a bore,
A whimsical dance, forevermore.

Voices Intertwined with the Wind

In the hollows, whispers twine,
As breezes tease the forest line.
Grass blades giggle, tickling toes,
While feathery shadows strike silly poses.

A brook babbles jokes, quite absurd,
Fish rolling eyes, not a single word.
Crickets chirp in comic refrain,
Nature's concert, no need for a chain.

Clouds drift in like jesters bold,
Spilling raindrops, stories untold.
They splash on puddles where giggles bloom,
Echoing laughter in nature's room.

The wind, a trickster, sweeps past my ear,
It tickles my thoughts, brings mirth and cheer.
And as I wander this merry way,
I'm bound to laugh, come what may.

www.ingramcontent.com/pod-product-compliance
Lightning Source LLC
Chambersburg PA
CBHW071854160426
43209CB00003B/545